CBT for Children and Adolescents

Evolutionary Guide That Helps To Manage Anxiety & Increase Self Esteem In Teenagers And Children

Cherilyn K. Chaffin

Table of Contents

INTRODUCTION 5

CHAPTER 1 6
WHAT'S COGNITIVE BEHAVIORAL THERAPY? 6
What does your client learn in CBT? 8

CHAPTER 2 10
COGNITIVE DISTORTIONS 10

CHAPTER 3 19
HOW IS CBT ADMINISTERED? 19
ADOLESCENT GROWTH GRADUATE 20

CHAPTER 4 25
COGNITIVE BEHAVIORAL THERAPY FOR ADOLESCENTS 25
Who Can Reap The Benefits Of Cognitive Behavioral Therapy? 26
Types of Cognitive Behavioral Therapy 27
Characteristics of Cognitive Behavior Therapies 35
The advantages of Cognitive Behavioral Therapy 38

CHAPTER 5 44
TEENAGER COGNITIVE BEHAVIORAL THERAPY (CBT) 44

CHAPTER 6 49
HOW COGNITIVE BEHAVIORAL THERAPY MIGHT ADVANTAGE YOUR TEEN. 49
The Basic Concepts of CBT 49

CHAPTER 7 55
EFFICACY FOR FEELING AND ANXIOUSNESS DISORDERS 55

CHAPTER 8 60
9 ESSENTIAL CBT TECHNIQUES AND TOOLS 60
9 Essential CBT Techniques and Tools infographic 65

Cognitive Behavioral Activities *84*
ACKNOWLEDGMENTS **91**

Copyright © 2020 by Cherilyn K. Chaffin

All rights reserved. No part of this publication may be reproduced, distributed, or transmitted in any form or by any means, including photocopying, recording, or other electronic or mechanical methods, without the prior written permission of the publisher, except in the case of brief quotations embodied in critical reviews and certain other non-commercial uses permitted by copyright law.

INTRODUCTION

This is a guide that will help you learn real strategies for overcoming obstacles and living the life they want using Cognitive Behavioral Therapy (CBT).

Each chapter presents key elements of CBT in clear, accessible language. Practical exercises are incorporated throughout, enabling you to practice and consolidate your learning. In addition, each chapter mimics the structure of an actual CBT session.

CHAPTER 1

What's Cognitive Behavioral Therapy?

Cognitive Behavioral Therapy (CBT) is a kind of psychotherapy that is utilized as an initial line treatment for a number of psychological and behavioral problems. It is an evidence-based therapy that is proven effective in dealing with depression, stress, eating disorders, drug abuse and many other mental disorders and behavioral problems.

CBT depends on the knowing that modifying maladaptive thoughts can result in positive changes in feelings and behavior. Its main concentrate is on your client all together, rather than specific disorders, to be able to recognize what thoughts and behaviors have to be fixed.

So how does CBT help?

In CBT the therapist helps your client or band of

clients to recognize current emotional and behavioral problems and change the thoughts and behaviors that cause them. Cognitive behavioral therapy posits that maladaptive thoughts, known as cognitive distortions, exacerbate and intensify psychological and behavioral problems. Cognitive distortions are exaggerated or irrational thought patterns that perpetuate unpleasant feeling says such as panic and depression.

A common exemplary case of a cognitive distortion is catastrophizing. Individuals who catastrophize expect the most severe to occur at every change or exaggerate the need for insignificant occasions. Catastrophizing leads us to think that things are much worse than they are actually, resulting in extreme dread and impaired decision making.

CBT helps your client by teaching them new and far better ways of considering themselves, their environment and current, recent and future life occasions. A client that is susceptible to catastrophizing would first be trained to note when the catastrophizing thoughts start to surface. Anxiety and stress are mitigated by considering other possible results and making a variation between a distressing event and a catastrophe. CBT also aids your client in developing skills for effectively dealing with stress and other life difficulties.

What does your client learn in CBT?

CBT can help your client figure out how to:

- Manage symptoms of mental illness.

- Prevent a relapse of mental disease or drug abuse.

- Use various approaches for dealing with stress and emotional pain.

- Effectively resolve interpersonal conflicts.

- Manage difficult feelings such as anger and sadness.

- Cope with stress or grief.

- Deal with a condition.

- Overcome anxiety and phobias.

- Replace maladaptive actions with healthy ones.

CHAPTER 2

Cognitive Distortions

Some of the most popular and effective Cognitive Behavioral Therapy techniques are put on what psychologist's call "cognitive distortions"

Cognitive distortions: inaccurate thoughts that reinforce negative thought patterns or emotions.

Cognitive distortions are defective ways that convince all of us of possibility that is merely not true.

You will find 15 main cognitive distortions that can plague even the most balanced thinkers sometimes:

- Filtering

Filtering identifies the way most of us can somehow disregard all the positive and good stuff inside our day to target solely on the negative. It could be much too easy to dwell about the same negative aspect, even though surrounded by a good number of good things.

- Polarized Thinking / "Dark and White" Thinking

This cognitive distortion is focused on seeing black and white only, without shades of grey. That is all-or-nothing considering, without room for difficulty or nuance. In the event that you don't perform properly in a few area, you might see yourself as a complete failure rather than simply unskilled in a single area.

- Overgeneralization

Overgeneralization is going for a solitary incident or time and utilizing it as the only real piece of proof for a wide general conclusion. For instance, a person may look for employment but have a negative interview experience, but rather than cleaning it off as a bad interview and attempting again, they conclude they are awful at interviewing and can never get employment offer.

- Jumping to Conclusions

Much like overgeneralization, this distortion involves defective reasoning in how exactly we make conclusions. Rather than overgeneralizing one event, however, jumping to conclusions identifies the inclination to make sure of something with no evidence whatsoever. We might be confident that someone dislikes us with only the flimsiest of evidence, or we might be convinced our fears should come true before we've an opportunity to find out.

- Catastrophizing / Magnifying or Minimizing

This distortion involves expectations that the worst may happen or has happened, predicated on hook incident that is nowhere close to the tragedy that it's made out to be. For instance, you can create a little mistake at the job and be persuaded that it'll ruin the task you will work on, your manager will be furious, and you'll lose your task. Alternatively, we might minimize the need for positive things, such as an achievement at the job or an appealing personal characteristic.

- Personalization

That is a distortion where a person believes that everything, they are doing has an effect on external events or other folks, no matter how irrational the hyperlink between. The individual experiencing this distortion will believe that they come with an unreasonably important role in the bad things that happen around them. For example, a person may think that the conference they were a few moments late in addressing was derailed because of these which everything could have been fine if indeed they were promptly.

- Control Fallacies

Another distortion involves feeling that everything that occurs to you is because exterior forces or credited to your own actions. Sometimes what goes on to us is because of causes we can't control, and sometimes what goes on is because of our actions, however the fake thinking is within assuming that it will always be one or the other. We might assume that the grade of our work is because of dealing with difficult people, or on the other hand that each mistake another person makes is because of something we do.

- Cognitive Distortions

- Fallacy of Fairness

We tend to be worried about fairness, but this concern can be studied to extremes. As we realize, life is not necessarily fair. The individual who undergoes life looking for fairness in every of their encounters will finish up resentful and unsatisfied. Sometimes things should go our way, and sometimes they'll not, it doesn't matter how fair it may look.

- Blaming

When things don't go our way, there are numerous

ways we can clarify or assign responsibility for the results. One technique of assigning responsibility is blaming others for what will go wrong. Sometimes we might blame others to make us feel or take action in a certain way, but this is a cognitive distortion because we will be the only ones accountable for just how we feel or work.

- Should

"Should" make reference to the implicit or explicit guidelines we have about how exactly we as well as others should behave. When others break our guidelines, we are annoyed. Whenever we break our very own guidelines, we feel guilty. For instance, we may come with an unofficial guideline that customer support representatives should be accommodating to the client. Whenever we interact with a person service representative that's not immediately accommodating, we may get angry. If we've an implicit rule that people are irresponsible if we purchase unnecessary things, we might feel exceedingly guilty whenever we spend even a little sum of money on something we don't need.

- Emotional Reasoning

This distortion involves convinced that if we feel a certain way, it must be true. For instance, if we feel unattractive or uninteresting in today's moment, we should be unattractive or uninteresting. This cognitive distortion comes right down to:

- "Personally, i think it, so that it must be true."

Clearly, our feelings aren't always indicative of the target truth, but it could be difficult to look earlier how exactly we feel.

Relevant: What's Emotional Cleverness? + 18 Methods to Improve It

- Fallacy of Change

The fallacy of change is based on expecting other

folks to improve as it suits us. This ties in to the feeling our joy depends on other folks, and their unwillingness or failure to improve, even if we drive and press and demand it, maintains us from being happy. That is obviously a damaging way to believe since nobody is accountable for our pleasure aside from us.

- Global Labeling / Mislabeling

This cognitive distortion can be an extreme form of generalizing, where we generalize a couple of instances or qualities into a worldwide judgment. For instance, if we fail at a particular task, we might conclude that people are an overall total failing in not only this area but every area. Alternatively, each time a stranger says something a little rude, we might conclude that she or he is an unfriendly person generally. Mislabeling is specific to using exaggerated and psychologically loaded vocabulary, such as saying a lady has abandoned her children when she leaves her children with a babysitter to relish a particular date.

- Always Being Right

While most of us enjoy being right, this distortion makes us think we should be right, that being wrong is unacceptable. We might think that being right is more important than the emotions of others, having the ability to admit when we've made a blunder or being reasonable and objective.

- Heaven's Incentive Fallacy

This distortion involves expecting that any sacrifice or self-denial on our part can pay off. We might think about this karma, and expect that karma will usually immediately incentive us for our good deeds. Obviously, this results in emotions of bitterness whenever we do not receive our prize.

Many tools and techniques within Cognitive Behavioral Therapy are designed to address or change these cognitive distortions.

CHAPTER 3

How is CBT administered?

Cognitive behavioral therapy is usually administered face-to-face in specific (private) sessions or in an organization. At Adolescent Development both methods are used. Clients receive person therapy 3 times weekly and go to CBT organizations six times weekly. They also take part in family therapy up to 2 times per week.

Our treatment team will start by gathering information about your client to be able to know what their major challenges and concerns are. This technique starts even before entrance through a pre-assessment evaluation which is completed by the client's main caregiver. Questions that are asked respect current and previous physical and psychological health, behaviors and previous life experiences.

One of the most crucial areas of administering

CBT, especially with youngsters, is creating a rapport. When your child strolls through the entrance way our personnel has begun interesting with them, learning them and creating a solid basis of empathy and trust:

"I have exposed to my therapist here as part of your before. I've distributed my joys, laughter and aches and pains and sorrows and I never experienced that I had not been accepted. That meant too much to me."

Adolescent Growth Graduate

Steps involved with CBT. There are many steps that happen in CBT. The order where they may be undergone is nonlinear and frequently some steps are repeated or revisited many times. These steps are the pursuing:

Identify resources of unpleasant feelings and stress.

Usually main steps in CBT is taking a look at your daily life and identifying major stressors. These range from things such as medical ailments, ongoing interpersonal issues, drug abuse issues, mental ailments, educational problems, divorce of parents or family problems, etc.

You as well as your therapist will spend some time collectively identifying and discussing areas of your life that are resources of stress and unpleasant feelings such as sadness, anger, anxiety, grief and dread. You might know entering therapy what your major stressors are, but sometimes new ones appear or are recognized as therapy proceeds.

Notice and describe your ideas, feelings and values about these stressors.

Your CBT therapist may request you to reflect on your daily life stressors and help you identify your primary thoughts, feelings and beliefs about them. Contrary to public opinion, this isn't an end alone. CBT is a useful and action-oriented treatment that targets determining problem, thoughts and behaviors and repairing them. This task is very important to helping you as well as your therapist hone in on the thoughts and values that donate to your struggling to be able to probe, restructure and change them.

Identify maladaptive or problematic thought patterns.

Your CBT therapist is keenly thinking about identifying the idea patterns that inform your emotional and behavioral problems. CBT is made upon the data that these problem patterns of considering are the reason behind maladaptive behavior and psychological pain.

Your therapist will encourage you to examine the beliefs you have determined as troublesome and problem them. That is a hard step, lots of the thoughts and values that are leading to your trouble are patterns of convinced experience ingrained in you for a long time. Perhaps these were discovered in child years or developed in response to an event you were not able to handle or process at that time.

It will cost significant amounts of your time and effort in CBT therapy focusing on this task. Your therapist realizes that it is simpler said than done and can afford you all their patience, empathy and understanding on the way.

Who can reap the benefits of CBT?

CBT has clinically been shown to be effective for a big quantity of mental and behavioral problems including:

- Depression.

- Anxiety.

- Eating disorders.

- Substance abuse.

- Co-occurring disorders.

- Bipolar disorder.

- Obsessive-compulsive disorder.

- Phobias.

- Post-traumatic stress disorder.

- Insomnia and sleep issues.

- ADD and ADHD

CHAPTER 4

COGNITIVE BEHAVIORAL THERAPY FOR ADOLESCENTS

During CBT sessions, patients are led toward a much better knowledge of the complex relationships which exist between thoughts, feelings and actions.

By better understanding the mental poison that lead to negative emotions and finally to negative behaviors, patients can understand how to change their perspectives to be able to improve their method of stressors in life and eventually make their own lives easier by modifying their behavior accordingly.

A teen's perspective of the world often contributes greatly to his actions and reactions as well as his day-to-day connection with others and himself. Learning how to identify how his perspective designs his experience in the world and exactly how moving those perspectives can completely alter his life is definitely an incredibly powerful and life-changing experience.

Learn more about how exactly cognitive behavioral therapy will benefit your child in recovery when you e- mail us at Muir Solid wood today.

Who Can Reap The Benefits Of Cognitive Behavioral Therapy?

Many adolescents who have problems with mental health disorders, addictions, and other issues can reap the benefits of cognitive behavioral therapy when it's an integral part of a thorough and intensive rehabilitation plan. Over time, research has demonstrated the efficacy of CBT over and over, which is commonly regarded as effective in the treating:

- Phobias

- Drug addiction

- Alcoholism

- Depression

- Anxiety

- Low self-esteem

- Self-harming behaviors

- Eating disorders

- Mood disorders

- Personality disorders

- Sleep disorders

- Psychotic disorders

- Obsessive-compulsive disorder

- Schizophrenia

Types of Cognitive Behavioral Therapy

It's important to comprehend that cognitive

behavioral therapy is not really a specific kind of therapy but instead a classification that encompasses an array of therapeutic interventions. A number of the restorative techniques that are one of these categories include:

- Rational emotive behavior therapy
- Rational behavior therapy
- Logical living therapy
- Cognitive therapy
- Dialectic behavior therapy
- Multimodal therapy
- Rational Emotive Behavior Therapy

Rational emotive behavior therapy was made in the 1950s with a psychologist named Alert Ellis; the treatment type was based, however, on the teachings of famous ancient and modern philosophers. While rational emotive behavior therapy is complex in nature, its definitive goal is to help people rid themselves of negative beliefs that lead to negative actions and also to replace those negative beliefs with positive ones that will, subsequently, lead to positive actions and a happier life generally

- Rational Behavior Therapy

Rational behavior therapy is comparable to the other styles of CBT except that its main focus is on locating the fundamental and unknown issues that are potentially accountable for the negative and unwanted mental, psychological or physical problems. Proponents of the therapy think that by finding and focusing on the underlying reason behind a person's problems, those problems can be solved, and the resulting negative feelings and interactions with others won't be a concern or as overwhelming to the individual.

- Rational Living Therapy

Logical living therapy combines both traditional therapy and self-counseling. In this kind of therapy, the therapist, known as a logical living therapist, efforts to "sell" your client on the techniques and strategies involved with logical living therapy.

Logical living therapists are persuasive and motivating toward their clients and present them clear directions to check out as they address underlying assumptions to be able to create long-term results. In addition they stay away from labeling patients with formal diagnoses when possible because they think that diagnoses can limit the patients they represent and lead them to feel hopeless.

- Rational Hypnotherapy

Some not absolutely all therapists who practice rational living therapy incorporate hypnotherapy to their classes. Why? Some possible benefits can include:

May assist in the faster integration of positive values and improved perspectives

May enhance the capability of the individual to totally embrace new ideas on the conscious level

May enhance the overall effectiveness of treatment through the excess repetition of the added layer of therapeutic intervention

Hypnotherapy is not essential for patients to reap the benefits of this kind of therapy; thus, therapists have the choice to learn in the technique or not.

- Cognitive Therapy

As is the situation with rational living therapy, cognitive therapy involves a therapist and a customer working closely jointly to perform predetermined therapeutic goals. The primary goal of the sessions is to recognize existing problems in the patient's life and also to disempower those problems by assisting the patient to get control over his thoughts, behaviors and emotional responses.

- Cognitive therapists first concentrate on educating the individual about his thoughts, feelings and actions, and exactly how each influences the other, before shifting to the development and practice of skills that will help to augment and enhance day-to-day experience.

- Dialectical Behavioral Therapy

Dialectical behavioral therapy typically utilizes a number of therapeutic methods including individual therapy sessions, group training and therapy sessions, and long-distance consultations when applicable. Another feature that sets dialectical behavioral therapy aside from other types of cognitive behavioral therapy is its great concentrate on validation and self-acceptance; the therapist helps the individual to simply accept his mental poison, feelings and actions. The theory is that by accepting problems in his life as the status quo, the individual will have a much greater potential for successfully conquering them and/or continue.

Many therapeutic programs that utilize dialectical behavioral therapy also concentrate on self-awareness and mindfulness through relaxation techniques such as yoga and meditation

The DRUG ABUSE and Mental Health Services Administration's Country with Registry of Evidence-Based Programs and Practices reduces dialectical behavior therapy into five components:

- Improving features of the individual through skills training
- Motivating the individual through the creation of the customized treatment plan
- Generalizing the knowledge of the individual in therapy to other facets of life
- Reinforcing adaptive behaviors

Implementing aid from a therapeutic team and consultation group

- Multimodal Therapy

Multimodal therapy targets seven key areas or the different parts of the personality and has shown very efficient in the treating children identified as having Attention Deficit and Hyperactivity Disorder (ADHD), though it could be applied in several different situations.

The American Psychological Association (APA) reports that the major foci of multimodal therapy are summed up by the acronym BASIC ID:

- Behavior: Problem behaviors

- Affect: Unpleasant emotions

- Feeling: Perceived psychosomatic problems

- Imagery: Negative self-image

- Cognition: Irrational thoughts

- Interpersonal factors: Nerve-racking relationships

- Drug/natural considerations: Biological disorders

Proponents of the treatment believe that it is essential to look for and treat issues that occur in each one of these areas, giving the individual the tools to recognize these issues and manage them as they arise.

Characteristics of Cognitive Behavior Therapies

Though each kind of cognitive behavior therapy differs and the specifics of therapeutic sessions will change depending upon the precise kind of therapy being practiced and the needs of the individual, all sorts of CBT share several common features. It really is these characteristics that define them as cognitive behavioral therapies, based on the Country wide Association of Cognitive Behavioral Therapists (NACBT). They may be:

- Predicated on the Cognitive Style of Emotional Response (e.g., the fact that thoughts, not outdoors occasions or circumstances, are what business lead to emotions and habits)

- A short-term intervention with a period limit positioned on treatment right away

- Predicated on a root belief in a solid however, not central therapist/client relationship

- Predicated on a root belief that both client and the therapist must interact toward problem-solving

- Predicated on stoic philosophy

- Focused on the use of the Socratic method (e.g., understanding clients' concerns through the requesting of questions and stimulating clients to ask "difficult questions" of themselves as well)

- Focused on the use of heavily organized therapeutic sessions

- Functional through the provision of clear directions to the individual

- Predicated on a root belief that emotional and behavioral reactions are discovered and can thus be unlearned

- Predicated on a focus on rational considering and perception of reality predicated on fact rather than emotion

Including "research" directed at the individual, or outdoors work that is usually to be completed by the individual among sessions

Children And Cognitive Behavioral Therapy

Cognitive behavioral therapy has definitely been shown to be particularly effective for use in treating adolescents and young adults.

This can be due partly to the actual fact that the feelings that rule most teens' decision-making processes and reactions never have been long used, thus they may be simpler to mold and form more positively in the therapeutic setting.

When data-driven, specific, and modified to

consider the precise needs of the individual and their developmental level, CBT can be extremely effective in the treating lots of diagnoses common in the teenager population, including:

- Depression
- Anxiety
- Eating disorders
- ADHD
- Substance abuse

However, it's important to keep in mind that whenever major disorders like those outlined are in evidence, an individual weekly therapy program is insufficient to combat the problem effectively. Rather, a treatment program that utilizes an array of traditional and alternative treatments will best serve to assist the individual in conquering problem issues and continue.

The advantages of Cognitive Behavioral

Therapy

When included as part of a thorough, teen-specific rehabilitation program, there are benefits to be enjoyed for teens who undergo cognitive behavioral therapy. A few of these benefits include:

- Improved communication skills
- Changes in negative thought patterns and resulting behaviors
- Improved ability to take care of worries and anxieties
- Lessening of addictive behaviors
- Lessening of self-destructive behaviors
- Increased self-esteem and self-confidence
- Improved sense of self
- Improved peer relationships

In general, young adults who complete a span of cognitive behavioral therapy can learn positive and appropriate approaches and approaches for coping with stress that serve to mitigate improper responses to stimuli.

Good Candidates for Cognitive Behavior Therapy

While nearly every adolescent can reap the benefits of cognitive behavioral therapy, certain characteristics and capabilities makes many people better applicants for an effective group of CBT periods than others, according to a report published in the Journal of Clinical Mindset.

A number of the features that can make a person more suitable for CBT and much more likely to reach your goals in their recovery are the following:

- An ability to identify, think about, and discuss the internal workings of your brain and thought processes
- The capability to establish specific goals for therapy
- A willingness to work toward recovery

- A desire to progress

- The capability to cope with an increase of emotional pain

- The capability to take ownership of certain problems in one's life

- The capability to learn and apply new information

- A well balanced, supportive home and family environment

Though many teens who start rehabilitation do not at first exhibit these qualities, many develop them throughout their time spent in a thorough program, making CBT very efficient when found in addition to other evidence-based therapies and therapeutic interventions.

Choosing a Cognitive Behavioral Therapy

It's important to be informed about the various types of cognitive behavioral therapy, but parents aren't tasked with identifying which kind will be most reliable for his or her child. Choosing if CBT will be a highly effective part of your teen's treatment solution, and if so, which kind comes after your son or daughter who undergoes an intensive preliminary evaluation. The healing team will determine which varieties of restorative intervention to make use of as they create a personalized treatment for your teen.

Finding Treatment For Your Child

There are a variety of characteristics which should define your teen's experience in rehabilitation. They include:

- A personalized treatment solution based on the average person needs of your son or daughter

- Directed therapeutic interventions chosen predicated on the impact they have on your child's ability to control all obstacles they face in recovery

- Addition of the parents and family in the healing process

- Teen-specific treatment

- Learn more about how exactly we can help your child cure when you e-mail us at Muir Real wood today. Get in touch with our call middle or download an admissions packet now.

CHAPTER 5

Teenager Cognitive Behavioral Therapy (CBT)

Teenager Cognitive Behavioral Therapy has been proven to have significant results on teens for several different issues, including however, not limited by: Feeling Disorders, Stress Disorders, Eating Disorders, and DRUG ABUSE struggles. Teenager Cognitive Behavioral Therapy is a goal-oriented method of therapy that targets examining cable connections between teenagers' thoughts, emotions, and behaviors. The target is to help teenagers improve thought patterns and behaviors that will subsequently supply them with rest from the negative symptoms related to Mental Health disorders. Teenager CBT is a little not the same as other kinds of therapy, for the reason that the therapists positively use the teenagers to conquer and/or decrease the symptoms associated using their current struggle. Instead of more general "Chat Therapy," CBT classes have more of the framework, as therapists intentionally guide teenagers to discuss and sort out specific topics and/or problems. The therapists consult with teenagers, the improvement they're making, as well as challenges they're still having, to constantly maintain a knowledge of the goals which have been arranged for the teenagers' treatment solution and where these are, along this route. This active involvement for the therapists also contains giving the teenagers "research" or exercises to apply beyond treatment sessions. As the therapy is dependant on the teenagers making changes in their own lives, this work must lengthen beyond just enough time while the teenagers are directly dealing with their therapist.

Because Teenager Cognitive Behavioral Therapy targets supporting teens to improve habits that are related to the challenges and symptoms they're experiencing, it's rather a very powerful tool in not only supporting the teenagers, but also help prevent relapse. A number of the useful steps that CBT might include into young treatment programs include adding positive activities to the teenagers' lives and restructuring negative and/or fake thought patterns.

CBT might be utilized to change teenagers' actions including things such as helping teenagers add positive, enjoyable activities to their daily lives. Though this might audio simple, it can frequently be very hard for teenagers who are depressed to really have the energy to start doing positive things for themselves, and likewise, it could be difficult for teenagers who are fighting Substance Abuse to include any "pleasant" activities that don't involve using.

Another concentrate of Young Cognitive Behavioral Therapy is to help young adults disrupt, and then restructure negative thought patterns. These negative self-perceptions and values often accompany virtually all Mental Health disorders, providing as the cause or result in negative behaviors and emotions. For instance, teenagers fighting Eating Disorders more often than not having problems with low self-esteem and many negative values about themselves, that leads them with their harmful behaviors. If teenagers are fighting Phobias or Anxiety Attacks, they have thought patterns set up that spiral uncontrollably. The difficult thing about these thought patterns is they could be very evasive to the teenagers' themselves, until they're motivated to really articulate the series of their thoughts with a therapist. Then, the contacts between one thought with another (or insufficient connection) becomes clearer. Therapists may then use the teenagers to disrupt these negative thought patterns from starting, the teenagers can start to regain a feeling of control over their thoughts, and for that reason, their emotions as well. This is often an extremely powerful step and can offer teens with substantial rest from what they're experiencing.

Research shows that Adolescent CBT can be a

very efficient therapeutic approach for several different Mental Health Disorders. Actually, it's been shown to be as effectual as medication treatment, for both Panic and Depression. Much like any remedy approach, certain teenagers will connect easier to CBT than others, but many teenagers enjoy and feel backed in the collaborative character of the particular technique and in addressing work actively using their therapist. In a lot as it is a short-term, rigorous, goal-oriented strategy, CBT can frequently be a great strategy to incorporate in your short-term home treatment programs at paradigm, alongside someone to other treatment approaches.

CHAPTER 6

How Cognitive Behavioral Therapy Might Advantage Your Teen

Cognitive behavioral therapy, also known as CBT, is a kind of psychotherapy that targets making connections between thoughts, behavior, and feelings. Psychotherapists who use CBT help people identify and change dysfunctional patterns.

CBT is often used in combination with adolescents. It could be effective in dealing with an array of issues including eating disorders, drug abuse, panic, and depression.

The Basic Concepts of CBT

CBT is dependent on the concept that there surely is a definite hyperlink between thoughts, behavior, and emotions. Here's a good example:

- Thought: I'm socially awkward

- Sense: Anxious

- Behavior: Teenager sits in the part only while at a celebration

A teenager who thinks she actually is awkward might avoid eye contact and shy from conversation. Then, when she does not have positive interpersonal interactions, her perception that she's socially uncomfortable is reinforced.

CBT goals to break that routine by changing just how a teen feels or behaves.

A psychotherapist can help the teenager problem negative assumptions with a behavioral test. For instance, the teenager who thinks she actually is socially uncomfortable might problem herself to hit up a discussion with five new people. If she encounters some success, her perception that she actually is socially uncomfortable is probably not as strong.

Additionally, the therapist can help her change her thoughts. When she tells herself, "People think I'm strange," she might remind herself, "Many people are different and that is Okay." Changing her thoughts can decrease the anxiety she encounters.

HOW IT OPERATES

Teenagers often develop distorted primary values about themselves. CBT helps confront and change those distortions.

A teenager who believes she's unworthy may always look for evidence that backs this belief up. For instance, if she gets a poor grade in the test, she may think it is because she's ridiculous. And if a pal doesn't call her back again, she may presume it is because her friend doesn't like her any longer.

A psychotherapist using CBT would help the individual identify those harmful thought patterns that donate to mental health issues. A therapist may ask some questions and have an individual to keep a thought record to help identify dysfunctional thoughts.

In later sessions, specific techniques are used that teach new ways to take into account maladaptive thought patterns and behaviors and could lead to far better means of getting one's needs met. For instance, CBT can succeed in treating a teenager with bulimia by discovering and assisting change thoughts, behaviour and feeling patterns about their body and food that leads to purging.

Benefits

CBT helps teenagers understand how to interpret their environment differently. In comparison to other restorative methods CBT is short-term. Sometimes, only a small number of classes are needed.

Additionally, it is very problem-focused, this means it handles into issues. Treatment providers aren't more likely to rehash a teen's years as a child or look for concealed indicating in their behavior. Instead, periods focus on assisting the teenager with problems happening now.

This sort of therapy can offer benefits such as:

- Improve communication with others
- Reduce fears and phobias
- Interrupt thoughts that lead to addictive or other self-destructive behaviors
- Improve self-esteem
- Identify positive responses to stress
- Change negative thought patterns

Where to find a Cognitive Behavioral Therapist

If your child is fighting a mental medical condition or a behavioral issue, speak to his doctor. Your physician can eliminate any possible medical issues, adding to the problem can send you to a cognitive behavioral therapist.

A cognitive behavioral therapist will probably want to interview you as well as your teen to get a better knowledge of the existing issue. Then, classes may include your child only or the therapist might want you or other family to attend.

CBT often involves research tasks. Getting parents involved with assisting a teen's attempts to complete the research can be key to improving. Make sure to speak to the therapist about how exactly you can best support your teen's treatment.

CHAPTER 7

Efficacy For Feeling And Anxiousness Disorders

Depression. A large number of Randomized Controlled Tests (RCT) and other studies support CBT's effectiveness in dealing with Major Depressive Disorder (MDD). For acute treatment:

• CBT works more effectively in producing remission in comparison to no treatment, treatment as typical, or non-specific psychotherapy.

• For slight to moderate despair, CBT is the same as antidepressant medication in conditions of response and remission rates.

• Merging antidepressant therapy with CBT raises treatment adherence.

Less popular may be a successful response to CBT in the acute stage may have a protective impact against unhappiness recurrences. A 2013 meta-analysis that totaled 506 people with depressive disorder found a pattern toward significantly lower relapse rates when CBT was discontinued after acute therapy, compared with anti-depressant therapy that continued beyond the acute phase.

Stress and anxiety. Among psychotherapies, CBT's superior efficiency for stress and anxiety disorders is well-established. CBT and its own specific-disorder adaptations are believed first-line treatment.

CBT's Essential Elements

CBT targets distorted cognitions about the personal, the world, and the near future, and on manners that business lead to or maintain symptoms.

Cognitive interventions seek to recognize thoughts and values that trigger psychological and behavioral reactions. A person with social panic, for example, might think that people will notice if he makes a good minor social mistake and then reject him, which can make him feel worthless. CBT can help him subject these beliefs to rational analysis and develop more adaptive beliefs, such as: "It isn't certain that I'll behave so badly that individuals would notice, but if that happened, the likelihood to be outright rejected is most likely low. If in the worst-case scenario I was rejected, I am not worthless; I'm only a fallible individual."

CBT's behavioral element can be conceptualized as Behavioral Activation (BA), a structured method of helping the individual:

• increase behaviors and encounters that are rewarding

• overcome obstacles to participating in these new behaviors

• and reduce behaviors that maintain symptoms.

BA can be considered a useful involvement for individuals with depressive disorder characterized by insufficient engagement or convenience of pleasurable encounters. During being pregnant and the postpartum period, for example, a female undergoes physical, cultural, and environmental changes that may gradually deprive her of resources of pleasure and other reinforcing activities. BA would concentrate on developing creative answers to regain usage of or create new opportunities for satisfying experiences and also to avoid behaviors (such as social withdrawal or exercise restriction) that perpetuate depressed mood.

Common elements. Cognitive and behavioral interventions concentrate on problem solving, individualized case conceptualization (Physique), and collaborative empiricism.

Individualized court case conceptualization lays the building blocks for the span of CBT, and could be regarded as a map for therapy. Case conceptualization earns several domains of assessment including symptoms and diagnosis, the patient's strengths, formative encounters (including biopsychosocial aspects), contextual factors, and cognitive factors that influence diagnosis and treatment, such as automated thoughts or schemas. The situation formulation leads to an operating hypothesis about the perfect course and focus of CBT.

Collaborative empiricism is how the individual and therapist interact to continually refine this working hypothesis. The set works together to research the hypotheses and every areas of the therapeutic romantic relationship.

CHAPTER 8

9 Essential CBT Techniques and Tools

There are numerous tools and techniques found in Cognitive Behavioral Therapy, a lot of that have spread from the treatment context to everyday living. The nine techniques and tools listed here are some of the most typical and effective CBT methods.

- Journaling

This system is a means of "gathering data" about our moods and our thoughts. This journal ranges from enough time of the feeling or thought, the foundation from it, the degree or strength, and how exactly we take care of it, among other factors. This Essential CBT Techniques and Tools technique can help us to recognize our thought patterns and psychological tendencies, explain them and discover how to improve, adapt, or deal with them.

- Unraveling Cognitive Distortions

This is a primary goal of CBT and can be practiced with or with no help of the therapist. To be able to unravel the cognitive distortions you possess, you must first notice which distortions you are most susceptible to. Part of these involves determining and challenging our dangerous automated thoughts, which frequently get into one of the categories outlined earlier.

- Cognitive Restructuring

Once you identify the distortions or inaccurate views on the world you possess, you can start to learn about how exactly this distortion took main and just why you came to trust it. When you find a perception that is harmful or dangerous, you can start to problem it. For instance, if you think that you'll want a higher paying job to be always a respectable person, nevertheless, you lose your high paying job, you will start to feel bad about yourself.

Rather than accepting this faulty belief leading you to believe unreasonably mental poison about yourself, you could take this chance to consider what makes a person "respectable," a belief you might not have explicitly considered before.

- Publicity and Response Prevention

This system is specifically effective for individuals who have problems with Obsessive Compulsive Disorder (OCD). You are able to practice this system by exposing you to ultimately whatever it is that normally elicits a compulsive behavior, but doing all your best to avoid the behavior and authoring it. You are able to combine journaling with this system, or use journaling to comprehend how this system enables you to feel.

- Interceptive Exposure

This technique is supposed to treat freak out. It involves contact with feared bodily feelings to be able to elicit the response, activates any unhelpful values from the feelings, maintains the feelings without distraction or avoidance, and invite new studying for the feelings to occur. It is designed to help the patient see that symptoms of stress aren't dangerous, although they might be uncomfortable.

- Nightmare Publicity and Rescripting

Nightmare publicity and rescripting are designed for those experiencing nightmares. This system is comparable to interoceptive publicity, for the reason that the headache is elicited, which introduces the relevant feelings. Once the feeling has arisen, your client and therapist interact to recognize the desired feelings and create a new image to accompany the required feeling.

- Play the Script Before End

This technique is particularly helpful for those experiencing anxiety and stress. In this system, the individual who's susceptible to crippling dread or stress conducts sort of thought test, where they imagine the results of the most severe case scenario. Allowing this situation play out can help the given individual to notice that even if everything they dread comes to move, it'll likely come out okay.

- Intensifying Muscle Relaxation (PMR)

That is a familiar strategy to those who practice mindfulness. Like the body scan, this system tells you to relax one muscle group at the same time until all of your person is in circumstances of Essential CBT Techniques and Tools relaxation. You should use audio assistance, a YouTube video, or just your own brain to practice this system, and it could be especially ideal for soothing nerves and calming an occupied and unfocused brain.

- Relaxed Breathing

That is another technique that's not specific to CBT but will be acquainted to practitioners of mindfulness. There are several ways to relax and bring regularity to your breathing, including led and unguided imagery, sound recordings, YouTube videos, and scripts. Getting regularity and relaxed to your breathing will help you to strategy your problems from a location of balance, facilitating far better and logical decision making.

These techniques can help those experiencing a variety of mental illnesses and afflictions, including anxiety, depression, OCD, and anxiety attacks, plus they can be practiced with or with no guidance of the therapist. To try a few of these techniques with no help of the therapist, start to see the next section for worksheets and handouts to aid with your practice.

9 Essential CBT Techniques and Tools infographic

If you're a therapist researching to guide your customer through treatment or a hands-on one who wants to learn by doing, there are numerous Cognitive Behavioral Therapy worksheets that will help.

- Alternate Action Formulation

This worksheet instructs an individual to first list any problems or difficulties you are experiencing. Next, you list your vulnerabilities (i.e., why you will experience these problems than another person) and causes (i.e., the stimulus or way to obtain these problems).

Once you've defined the issues and realize why you are fighting them, you continue to list coping strategies. They are not answering to problems, but ways that you can offer with the consequences of those issues that can have a short-term impact. Next, you list the consequences of the coping strategies, such as the way they cause you to feel in the short-term and long-term, and advantages and drawbacks of every strategy.

Finally, you move to listing alternative actions. In case your coping strategies aren't totally effective against the issues and troubles that are occurring, you are instructed to list other strategies that are better.

This worksheet gets you (or your client) considering what you are really doing now and whether it's the simplest way forward.

This worksheet will be accessible for download soon.

- Functional Analysis

One popular technique in Cognitive Behavioral Therapy in functional evaluation. This technique can help you (or your client) find out about yourself, specifically what leads to specific behaviors and what effects derive from those behaviors.

In the center of the worksheet is a package tagged "Behaviors." With this package, you jot down any possibly problematic behaviors or other behaviors you intend to analyze.

On the remaining side of the worksheet is a package labeled "Antecedents," where you or your client jot down the factors that preceded a specific behavior. They are factors that led up to the behavior in mind, either straight or indirectly.

Around the right part is the ultimate container, labeled "Consequences." That's where you jot down the results of the behavior, or what occurred consequently of the behavior in mind. "Effects" may audio inherently negative, however they are not always negative; some positive outcomes can occur from various kinds of behaviors, even if more negative implications result as well.

This worksheet will help you or your client to discover whether particular behaviors are adaptive and helpful in striving towards your targets, or destructive and self-defeating.

This worksheet will be accessible for download soon.

- Longitudinal Formulation

This worksheet can help you address what some Cognitive Behavioral Therapy therapists call the

"5 P Factors" - presenting, predisposing, precipitating, perpetuating, and positives. This formulation process will help you connect the dots in the middle of your primary values and thought patterns as well as your present behavior.

This worksheet presents five boxes near the top of the page, that ought to be completed before shifting to all of those other worksheets.

The first box is labeled "Precipitating Events / Triggers," and corresponds with the Precipitating factor. Within this package, you are instructed to jot down the occasions or stimuli that provoke a certain behavior.

Another box is labeled "Early Experiences" and corresponds to the Predisposing factor. That's where you list the encounters you had earlier on, completely back to child years, that may have added to the behavior.

The 3rd box is "Core Values," which is also related to the Predisposing factor. That's where you jot down a few of the relevant primary values you have regarding this behavior. They are values that might not be explicit, but that you think deep down, such as "I'm bad" or "I'm inadequate."

The fourth box is "Old Guidelines for Living," which is where you list the guidelines that you abide by, whether consciously or subconsciously. These implicit or explicit guidelines can perpetuate the behavior, even if it's not helpful or adaptive. Guidelines are if-then claims offering a judgment predicated on a couple of circumstances. For example, you might have the guideline "EASILY do not take action perfectly, I'm an entire failure."

The ultimate box is labeled "Presenting Problems / Ramifications of Old Guidelines." That's where you jot down how well these guidelines will work for you. Are they assisting you to be the best you will be? Are they assisting you to effectively strive towards your targets?

Below this container, there are two circulation charts that you can complete based about how these behaviors and emotions are perpetuated. You are instructed to think about a predicament that produces a poor automated thought and record the feelings and the behavior that thought provokes, as well as the physical feelings that can result. Filling in these movement charts will help you see what drives your behavior or thought and what results from it.

Below both of these charts is the package "Protective Factors." That's where you list the factors that will help you offer with the problematic behavior or thought, as well as perhaps help you break the perpetuating routine. This are things that help you deal after the thought or behavior occurs or things that can disrupt the design once it is within motion.

Finally, the last box is "New Rules for Living." This container pertains to the Positive factor, for the reason that it offers you with a chance to create new guidelines for yourself that will disrupt the destructive routine and invite you to be far better in getting together with your therapeutic goals.

This worksheet will be accessible for download soon.

Dysfunctional Thought Record

This worksheet is particularly helpful for individuals who are fighting mental poison and need to determine when and just why they are likely to pop-up. By learning more in what provokes certain automated thoughts, they become simpler to address and invert.

The worksheet is split into seven columns:

Within the far still left, there is certainly space to jot down the day and time when a dysfunctional thought arose.

The next column is where in fact the situation is detailed. An individual is instructed to spell it out the function that led up to the dysfunctional thought at length.

The 3rd column is perfect for the automated thought. That's where the dysfunctional automated thought is documented, plus a ranking of perception in the idea on the level from 0% to 100%.

Another column is where in fact the emotion or feelings elicited by this thought are shown, also with a rating of intensity on the scale from 0% to 100%.

The fifth column is tagged "Distortion." This column is where in fact the consumer will identify which cognitive distortion(s) they suffer from in relation to this type of dysfunctional thought, such as all-or-nothing considering, filtering, jumping to conclusions, etc.

The next to last column is perfect for the user to jot down alternative thoughts, more positive and functional thoughts that can replace the negative one.

Finally, the last column is perfect for the user to jot down the end result of the exercise. Were you in a position to confront the dysfunctional thought? Do you jot down a convincing option thought? Do your perception in the idea and/or the strength of your feeling(s) decrease?

Truth or Opinion

One of the best Cognitive Behavioral Therapy worksheets is the "Reality or Opinion" worksheet since it can be hugely helpful in recognizing that your ideas aren't necessarily true.

Near the top of this worksheet can be an important lesson:

Thoughts aren't facts.

Of course, it could be hard to simply accept this, particularly when we are in the throes of the dysfunctional thought or extreme emotion. Filling in this worksheet will help you come to the realization.

This simple exercise can help an individual to see that while we've lots of emotionally charged thoughts, they aren't all objective truths. Realizing the difference between truth and opinion can help us in challenging the dysfunctional or dangerous opinions we've about ourselves as well as others.

This worksheet will be accessible for download soon.

- Cognitive Restructuring

This worksheet employs the utilization of Socratic questioning, a method that will help an individual to challenge irrational or illogical thoughts.

The very best of the worksheet describes how thoughts are a running dialogue inside our minds, plus they will come and go so fast that people hardly have time to handle them. This worksheet seeks to help us catch a couple of the thoughts and analyze them.

The first box to be done is "Thoughts to be questioned." That's where you jot down a particular thought, usually, one you think is destructive or irrational.

Next, you jot down the data for and from this thought. What proof is there that the thought is accurate?

Once you've identified the data, you may make a view upon this thought, specifically whether it's predicated on facts or your emotions.

Next, you answer a question on whether this thought is actually a dark and white situation, or whether reality leaves room for tones of grey. That's where you see whether you are employing all-or-nothing considering, or making things unreasonably simple when they may be truly complex.

Within the last package upon this page, you take into account whether you will be misinterpreting the data or making any unverified assumptions.

On another web page, you are instructed to take into account whether other folks may have different interpretations of the same situation, and what those interpretations might be.

Next, consider whether you are considering all the relevant evidence or simply the data that backs up the perception you already keep. Make an effort to be as goal as possible.

Another box asks you whether your thought may have an exaggeration of the truth. Some mental poison are located in truth but prolonged past their reasonable boundaries.

Next, you are instructed to consider whether you are entertaining this negative considered habit or because the reality truly support it.

Once you've decided if the facts support this thought, you should think about how exactly this thought came for you. Was it offered from another person? If so, are they a trusted source for truth?

Finally, you complete the worksheet by identifying how likely the scenario your thought introduces happens to be, and whether it's the most severe case scenario.

These "Socratic questions" encourage a deep dive

in to the thoughts that may plague you, and provide a chance to analyze and evaluate them for truth. If you're having thoughts that do not result from a location of truth, this worksheet can be a great tool for determining and defusing them.

Even More CBT Interventions And Exercises

Haven't experienced enough CBT tools and techniques yet? Keep on to get more useful and effective exercises!

- Behavioral Experiments

They are related to thought tests, for the reason that you take part in a "imagine if" concern. Behavioral tests change from thought tests in that you really try these "what ifs" beyond your ideas

To be able to test a thought, you can test out the final results that different thoughts produce. For instance, you can attempt the idea:

"EASILY criticize myself, I am motivated to work harder" vs. "EASILY is kind to myself, I am motivated to work harder.

First, you'll try criticizing yourself if you want the inspiration to work harder and record the results. You then would try being kind to yourself and documenting the results. Next, you'll compare the leads to see which thought was nearer to the truth.

- These behavioral experiments will help you understand how to best strive communicate therapeutic goals as well as how to be your very best self.

- Thought Records

Thought records are of help in screening the validity of your ideas. They involve gathering and analyzing the data for and against a specific thought, enabling an evidence-based summary on if the thought is valid or not.

You can even try scheduling a task for every day that delivers you with a feeling of mastery or accomplishment. It's great to take action pleasurable, but doing something small that can cause you to feel achieved may have more durable and farther achieving effects.

This simple technique can introduce more positivity into your entire day and help you create your thinking less negative.

Imagery Based Exposure

This exercise involves considering a recently available memory that produced strong negative feelings and analyzing the problem.

For instance, if you recently had a battle with your spouse plus they said something hurtful, you may bring that situation to brain and make an effort to remember it at length. Next, you'll make an effort to label the feelings and thoughts you experienced through the situation and identify the urges you experienced (e.g., to hightail it, to yell at the spouse, to cry).

Visualizing this negative situation, specifically for a long-term time frame, can enable you to eliminate its ability to induce you and reduce avoidance coping. When you expose you to ultimately all the emotions and urges you sensed in the problem and survive exceptional memory, it requires a few of its power away.

Situation Publicity Hierarchies

This system may sound complicated, but it's not at all hard.

Situation Publicity Hierarchies involves making a summary of things that you'll normally avoid. For instance, someone with severe interpersonal panic may typically avoid making a telephone call rather than emailing or requesting someone on the date.

Next, you rate each item about how distressed you think you'd be, on a level from 0 to 10, if you involved in it. For the individual experiencing severe social anxiousness, asking someone on the time may be ranked a 10 on the size, while making a telephone call rather than emailing might be graded nearer to a three or four.

Once you've rated each item, you rank them according with their stress rating. This can help you identify the biggest problems you face, which can help you select what to address and in what order. It might be best to begin with the less distressing items and work the right path up to the most distressing items.

Situation Publicity Hierarchies CBT Interventions and Exercises

If you're thinking about giving CBT a go with your clients, there are extensive books and guides that will help get you started. A few of these books are for the therapist only, plus some should be navigated as a team or with assistance from the therapist.

There are various manuals away there for helping therapists apply Cognitive Behavioral Therapy in their work, but they are a few of the most popular:

- A Therapist's Guide to Short Cognitive Behavioral Therapy

- Person Therapy Manual for Cognitive-Behavioral Treatment of Depression.

- Provider's Guidebook: "Activities as well as your Feeling"

- Treatment Manual for Cognitive Behavioral Therapy for Depressive disorder

For clients or for therapist and customer to sort out together, they are a few of the most popular guides and workbooks:

- The CBT Toolbox: A Workbook for Clients and Clinicians.

- Client's Guidebook: "Activities as well as your Disposition.

- The Cognitive Behavioral Workbook for Anxiety: A Step-by-Step Program

- The Cognitive Behavioral Workbook for Major depression: A Step-by-Step Program

- Cognitive-Behavioral Therapy Skills

Workbook

There are a great many other manuals and workbooks away there that will help get you started with Cognitive Behavioral Therapy, but they are an excellent start.

Cognitive Behavioral Activities

Before we go, there are many more Cognitive Behavioral Therapy activities and exercises which may be ideal for you or your clients that we'd prefer to cover.

- Mindfulness Meditation

As readers of the blog will probably know right now, mindfulness can have an array of positive impacts, including helping with depression, anxiety, addiction, and a great many other mental illnesses or difficulties.

Mindfulness can help those experiencing harmful automated Cognitive Behavioral Activities thoughts to disengage from rumination and obsession of these thoughts by supporting them, stay firmly grounded in todays.

- Successive Approximation

That is a somewhat fancy name for a straightforward proven fact that you have likely already heard about: splitting up large tasks into small making it simpler to accomplish.

It could be overwhelming to be confronted with an enormous goal we wish to perform, like opening a company or remodeling a residence. That is true in mental health treatment as well, because the goal to conquer depression or stress and anxiety and achieve mental wellbeing can seem just like a monumental job to those who find themselves experiencing severe symptoms.

By breaking the large goal into small, easy to perform steps, we can map out the road to success and make the trip seem just a little less overwhelming.

Writing Self-Statements To Counteract Mental

Poison

This system can be problematic for someone just beginning their Cognitive Behavioral Therapy treatment or experiencing severe symptoms, but it may also be very efficient

When you (or your customer) are suffering from negative thoughts, it could be hard to confront them, particularly if your perception in these thoughts is strong. To counteract these mental poisons, it could be helpful to jot down a positive, reverse thought.

For instance, if the idea that you will be worthless keeps popping into your mind, try recording a declaration like "I am a person with well worth" or "I am a person with potential." Initially, it could be difficult to simply accept these alternative thoughts, however the more you draw out these positive thoughts to counteract the negative ones, the more powerful the association will be.

- Visualize the very best Elements of Your

Day

If you are feeling depressed or negative, it is difficult to identify that there surely is good in your daily life as well. This simple technique of getting to mind the nice areas of your entire day can be a little part of the path of realizing the positive

All you have to do is jot down the items in your daily life that you will be most thankful for or things that are most positive in your entire day. The simple take action of recording these good stuffs can forge new organizations in your thoughts which will make it simpler to start to see the positive, even though there is enough of negative as well.

- Reframe Your Mental Poison

It could be all too easy to succumb to mental poison as a default environment. When you are immediately thinking a poor thought when you see something new, such as getting into a new room and considering "I hate the colour of that wall structure," give reframing a go

Reframing requires countering the negative thought(s) by noticing things you are feeling positive about as fast as possible. For example, in the example where you immediately think of how much you hate the colour of that wall structure, you would drive you to ultimately notice five things in the area that you are feeling favorably about (e.g., the carpet appears comfortable, the lampshade is fairly, the home windows let in a great deal of sunlight).

You are able to set your telephone to remind you during the day to stop what you are really doing and think of the positive things around you. This assists you to press your thoughts back to the world of the positive rather than the negative.

cognitive behavioral activities

You are able to download the printable version of the infographic here.

As always, I am hoping this post has been helpful. There are a great number of great tips and techniques in here that may be very efficient in the fight against depression, nervousness, OCD, and a bunch of other problems or issues.

However, as is the situation numerous treatments, they depend on you (or your client) investing in a lot of work. I'd encourage you to provide these techniques a genuine try, and invite yourself the blissful luxury of considering if they could actually work. Whenever we strategy a potential solution with the assumption that you won't work, then it'll most likely not work. Whenever we strategy a potential solution with an open up mind and the idea that it might just work, they have a far greater chance of being successful.

If you are fighting negative automated thoughts, please contemplate these pointers and techniques and present them a genuine shot. Similarly, if your customer is struggling, cause them to take the time, because the payoff can be much better than they can see right now.

Acknowledgments

The Glory of this book success goes to God Almighty and my beautiful Family, Fans, Readers & well-wishers, Customers and Friends for their endless support and encouragements.

www.ingramcontent.com/pod-product-compliance
Lightning Source LLC
Chambersburg PA
CBHW020301030426
42336CB00010B/863